POETRY ORIGINALS

Nearly Thirteen

Other Poetry Originals

The Magnificent Callisto *Gerard Benson*
Two's Company *Jackie Kay*
Grandad's Seagulls *Ted Walker*

SERIES EDITOR: ANNE HARVEY

POETRY ORIGINALS

Nearly Thirteen

by Jan Dean

Illustrated by Debi Ani

Blackie Children's Books

BLACKIE CHILDREN'S BOOKS
Published by the Penguin Group
Penguin Books Ltd, 27 Wrights Lane, London W8 5TZ, England
Penguin Books USA Inc., 375 Hudson Street, New York, New York 10014, USA
Penguin Books Australia Ltd, Ringwood, Victoria, Australia
Penguin Books Canada Ltd, 10 Alcorn Avenue, Toronto, Ontario, Canada M4V 3B2
Penguin Books (NZ) Ltd, 182–190 Wairau Road, Auckland 10, New Zealand

Penguin Books Ltd, Registered Offices: Harmondsworth, Middlesex, England

First published 1994
1 3 5 7 9 10 8 6 4 2
First edition

Text copyright © Jan Dean, 1994
Illustrations copyright © Debi Ani, 1994

The moral right of the author has been asserted

All rights reserved. Without limiting the rights under copyright reserved above, no part of this publication may be reproduced, stored in or introduced into a retrieval system, or transmitted, in any form or by any means (electronic, mechanical, photocopying, recording or otherwise), without the prior written permission of both the copyright owner and the publisher of this book

Filmset in Palatino by
Rowland Phototypesetting Ltd
Bury St Edmunds, Suffolk
Printed and bound in Great Britain by
Butler & Tanner Ltd, Frome and London

A CIP catalogue record for this book is available from the British Library

ISBN 0-216-94066-4

For Peter and Maureen Maybank

Contents

Introduction   9

The Unit of Sleep	15
Playschool	16
Stupid	18
Play Green	19
Not Now, I'm Working	21
Symptoms	22
First Time	23
Second Time	25
Gone	26
Hat Hokey Cokey	27
Blue	29
Girl in the Library	30
Sideways	31
Approximate Frog	32
Horror	33
Meltis	35
Big Fish	37
Windows	39
Elephant	40
Tramp	41
Fat Ladies in the Cinema	42
Aunt Ellen's Bed	44
Waiting For	45
Edward	46
The Unlucky Baker	48
Roy's Dance	49
Ghosts in Our Suburban Homes	51
No More Socks	53
Advice to the Horticulturalist	54

The Seven Brains of the Caterpillar	56
Marcello Malpighi's Theory	57
The Barber-Surgeon at Avebury	58
Holme Fen	63
Choosing	65
Sunday School Sports	66
Olympic Diver	67
Uniform	68
Nearly Thirteen	69
The Jam and Bread Test	71
Barbara in the Shed	72
In the Meantime	73
A Serious Talk	74
Heart Stuff	77
Angels	79

Introduction

On an April evening in 1991 I came home after a poetry event with the words of one of the day's poems running through my head . . .

> That wasn't how it happened . . .
> We never meant to lock her in
> The door stuck. I was playing with the bolt.

The poem had character, pace and energy, and so did the poet, Jan Dean. Soon afterwards we met again, and that meeting led to this collection for Poetry Originals. You can read that poem, 'Barbara in the Shed', later in this book.

Jan Dean, you'll discover, has unusual and varied ideas on many subjects. She likes to explore the unknown, the area of 'What if . . . ?' or 'Suppose . . . ?' Her imagination is fired by the past, by scientific thought, by the fantastic, but she can be equally inspired by everyday happenings and the incidents and feelings of her own childhood. Jan was adopted when she was a tiny baby, and from the beginning was told the story of how her parents chose her rather than a red-haired baby boy. She tells of this in her poem,

'Choosing'. Childhood was happy, especially inside, at home; the outside world could sometimes be lonely, but this, she told me, sent her 'into my head, and to books, always books'. It was her mother who passed on to her the gift of storytelling. Her parents kept a grocer's shop in Stalybridge, once a Cheshire mill-town, and Jan believes that shop life permanently affected the way she speaks to people. 'It's given me this built-in feeling of being here to do something for people . . . to help them . . . it's turned me into one of life's volunteers.' Perhaps this is why she always draws a smiling face after signing her name!

Sometimes Jan was allowed to help in the shop, and a favourite job was scooping the dark, shiny, aromatic coffee beans from sacks into tins. Once, sent to fetch some bottles of Corona from the cellar, she saw

> . . . Two long pale frogs. Glistening.
> Jewels on the dark stone flags . . .

Unexpected and alarming to a young child at the time, it has emerged later as the subject for one of her most vivid poems, 'Horror', included in this book.

Jan was quite young when she heard about a local poet, Samuel Laycock, who had lived in Victorian times and written in dialect. She learnt some of his poems, like this sad one about a poor family's new baby, 'Welcome Bonny Brid':

> Th'art welcome, little bonny brid
>   But shouldn't ha' come just when tha did;
>   Toimes are bad.
> We're short o' pobbies for eawr Joe,
>   But that, of course, tha didn't know,
>   Did ta, lad?

The shape of those dialect words, the sounds and rhythm, were to stay with her, and she liked the idea that poets could live in an ordinary place as she did.

Passing the 11-plus exam led to big changes in Jan's life. She had to travel by bus to Astley County Grammar School in Dukinfield, but although this meant seeing less of her Stalybridge friends the new school brought new experiences. Biology became one of her favourite subjects, and with the excellent teaching of two English teachers, Mrs Proctor and Miss Parks, Jan entered another world . . . that of literature. These two teachers developed her love of stories, legends and the Greek myths as well as her enjoyment of writing. She remembers one character at the school, an eccentric French master who played his violin in the lunch hour, clad in overcoat and scarf, while waiting for a pupil – often Jan – to bring the bowl of rice pudding prescribed for his ulcer. I expect to see a poem about him one day.

After training as a teacher, Jan taught English and Drama and began to write seriously, attending courses and workshops. It was during this time that an English adviser in Northumberland heard one of her poems on the radio, got in touch with her through the BBC and invited her to read at a teachers' meeting. This real encouragement was a turning point for Jan, and changed the way she saw herself. Her writing took a big step forward from which she never looked back . . . so it seems right that this collection should take the title of that poem, 'Nearly Thirteen', and be dedicated to the English adviser and his wife, who became Jan's close friends.

Jan and her husband, John, with their sons, Matthew and Christopher, live in an old cottage in the middle of a Surrey town. Their home is full of colour and activity, toys and flowers and books, and the boys' pictures on the walls. When I visited I was greeted with the smell of fresh baked herb and cheese bread. Jan's first book, an adventure story called *The Fight for Barrowby Hill*, came out last year. This year two more are to be published, a light-hearted one called *Me, Duncan and the Great Hippopotamus Scandal* and a serious thriller called *Finders*.

Every editor dreams of finding a new and original poet and for me it's been especially exciting to discover Jan Dean, who 'measures fun in grandads', who 'is sick of socks', and instead demands . . . 'an earthquake . . . wrapped in lava glittery as foil and bright as marmalade'; a poet who tells her readers to

Spread the rainbow message round the world
A hundred thousand times.
Plant a seed and raise a forest
Hear the bluebell when it chimes.

Explode all the colours you've ever seen,

            THINK PINK
  and   PLAY GREEN!

ANNE HARVEY

The Unit of Sleep

I measure fun in grandads –
The best slide in the park is three whole
 grandads long.

I measure ponds in duckfuls –
This is a lake. Tons of ducks. Swans. Green
 mud, good pong.

Picnics are weighed in chocolate biscuits.
Don't care if they do melt, so long as there's
 a lot.

Holidays stretch in yards of sunshine.
Sand, seaslap, shingle. Donkey smell and
 leather. Hot.

Journeys are timed in songs and stories –
From here to Aunt Em's house the wicked
 witch schemes
And as we arrive there the Prince rescues
 Snow White.

The unit of sleep is dreams.

Playschool

'S got glue in it
and goo in it
crayons and paints and seeds that we grew
  in it.

'S got cake in it
stuff we make in it
things that we play with (and chuck round
  and break) in it.

'S got fish in it
gunge that goes squish in it
frocks to dress up be whatever you wish in
  it.

'S got my friends in it
odds and ends in it
good junk with twiddly wire bits to play
  mend in it.

'S got books in it
nosh we cooks in it
Sneaky Pete crafty crannies with nooks in it.

'S got wood in it
got grass with mud in it
I'd stay here for ever, if I could in it.

Oo it's GOOD, innit?

Stupid

My friends are stupid
My teacher's stupid
But I'm not stupid.

The weather's stupid
My coat is stupid
But not me. Oh, not me.

My shoes are stupid
My sticky bedroom door is stupid
This stupid bike with its stupid flat tyre is
    stupid
And my stupid granny who knitted this
    stupid scarf
That keeps dangling in this stupid puddle is
    stupid
And I want my stupid mum!

Play Green

Out of the big brown belly of the ground
A long green finger grew. Next came a sound.
A great green voice boomed – echoed through the town –
Take the stripes of the rainbow and throw them all around!
Come on attack black tarmac!
Away grey clay!
Find the hidden rainbows in the corners of the day.
Dance all the colours you've ever seen,

           THINK PINK
  and   PLAY GREEN!

Hullaballoo BLUE.
Dream-in-your-bed RED.
If you give up on the rainbow you might as well be dead.
Sing all the colours you've ever seen,

           THINK PINK
  and   PLAY GREEN!

Paint a turtle purple
And a wild moose puce.
Make a hairy hornet yellower
With yellow melon juice.
Zoom with all the colours you've ever seen,

                THINK PINK
    and   PLAY GREEN!

Do a hugger-mugger juggle with oranges and limes
Be a multi-coloured acrobat who balances on rhymes
Spread the rainbow message round the world
A hundred thousand times.
Plant a seed and raise a forest
Hear the bluebell when it chimes.

Explode all the colours you've ever seen,

                THINK PINK
    and   PLAY GREEN!

Not Now, I'm Working

My mother dressed is sharp and neat
With everything in place, each pleat
And tuck a knife-edge crease.
My mother dressed is orderly, in charge,
And nothing beats her. Nothing large
Or difficult defeats her.

But mother in her bed is something else
A sweet and talcumed, casually amalgamed,
Gentle rearrangement of soft domes.
Without the rigid armour of the day
She sleeps. And in the morning when I play
And climb into the big bed, she's not too
  busy,
Not too full of jobs. It's when she's dressed
That she sends me away.

Symptoms

A mump. A single lop-sided lump
Sits in my neck like a granite egg.

Don't swallow, oh no, don't –
A gulp sets loose a turbulence of gravel,
A fizz of gritty bees
Of wasps within the tender place
Where ear meets throat.

I am the python who guzzled the hive
The ostrich who gobbled the hedgehog.

First Time

My dad's in the pantomime.
My dad is a star.
My dad's better than your dad
And funnier by far.
My dad tells the best jokes
My dad sings great songs
My dad's in the wings now
He's coming. Won't be long.

My dad doesn't look right
My dad's not like that
He doesn't have long hair at home
That's not his proper hat.
He doesn't have big bright red lips
Or bosoms like balloons.
I want my dad back like he was.
I want to go home. Soon.

Why did no one tell me
That he'd be in disguise?
I think it's sort of scarey;
I know they're my dad's eyes,
But who's the face they're peeping from?
And whose the painted grin?
Whose is the huge black beauty spot
Upon his powdered chin?
My dad's mixed up with other bits
Of people I don't know.
He's chopped and changed.
All rearranged. Down in the second row
I howl. My father's lost.

This pantomime's a monster,
Don't believe its jolly song.
The panto ate my father
Then spat him out all wrong.
I hate the bouncy dancers
Tap-tapping in a line.
This pantomime's pretending
Its smile is Frankenstein.

Second Time

My dad wears purple earrings.
My dad wears ruffled frocks.
My dad wears sequinned underwear
And amazing spotty socks.

Some fathers go canoeing.
Some fathers write and rhyme.
Some fathers can build bookshelves.
Mine's a dame in pantomime.

Gone

The photograph is black and white
But I remember that the dress was purple
That the hair was red and matted as an old
 dead fox.
My dad in pantomime. A tall thin ugly sister.

Bennett Street could do a panto
Good as any at the Palace or the Hipp.
There were huntsmen dancing in red silk
And princes dressed in satin skies and stars.

Then the place closed down.
They shut the Sunday School,
Dug up the old bones in the graveyard
And built a supermarket.

So all that's left of glory
Is a box of stuff. An old black bag of
 costumes
Not for Crusoe or for Whittington
Just rags for dressing up.

Hat Hokey Cokey

She put my hat right on,
I took my hat right off,
On, off. On, off.
I don't care if I cough.
I don't care if I catch the flu
The ague or the plague
This hat is staying off!

Oh-oh I hate my brown hat.
Oh-oh I hate my red hat.
Oh-oh that's what I said, hat,
Slip-tip you out of sight.

You put that hat back on.
Just put that hat back on.
Off! On! Off! On –
Until your cold is gone!
You've got to keep your head warm
So you'll wear your hat.
And that, my girl, is flat.

Oh-oh I hate my brown hat,
Oh-oh I hate my blue hat,
Oh-oh what shall I do, hat?
Stuff-stick you in the bin!

It makes my head too hot
It makes me itch a lot
Itch scratch, itch scratch
I've rubbed a red raw patch
I hate all hats that tickle
Hats that make me squirm
Hats knitted out of worms!

Oh-oh I loathe my brown hat,
Oh-oh I loathe my green hat,
Oh-oh you wriggly mean hat,
SNIP-RIP! You're all in bits!

Blue

No one understood why he was blue
Although he came from Somerset, he said.
Down there they're not like us. Who knows?
He was a cyanotic shade. The colour of the
  murdered dead.
At any rate he was unhappy here in Wigan.
The bedsit was too small, too warm, too dry
Too lined with dusty books. Too full of
  visitors
And beer. He longed for home,
Would linger on the landing. He began
To loiter in the bathroom. Very sly.
He liked the clammy condensation. Clung to
  damp
Cold towels and the slime that gathered at
  the plug.
He died there – where he'd felt the tug of old
  times.
Where the cistern boomed
Much like the voice of his old master
  through the mist –
The vapour rising, dripping like the vaults
  and crypts
He'd left behind and never ceased to miss.

Girl in the Library

Pores over star maps
Like a sailor;
Behind her great iron pillars
Twist like barleysugar
To the pitched white roof
That keeps her from the sky.
Before her the staircase
Corkscrews into ground
She cannot leave.
She leafs longingly through galaxy and
 galaxy
While solid stones of all around
Slur and diffuse – unfold like petals
Or slow milk clouds in tea.
The library is melting as she reads,
Like time-lapse film of rain storms
      clustering/blossoming
      clustering/blossoming
Space and space and million-studded space.

Sideways

They were not tadpoles in the snow
– for all their blackness
and their stillness, frozen
mid-squirm in the inch thick fall.

They were not tadpoles
underneath the kitchen window
black and still
– caught in the untoward and frozen by a look.

Not mistimed plagues
en route for Egypt
hoping to be ripe and green enough
to fall on Pharaoh,
but seeds blown down
from the high dark branches

lying where a month or so ago
the leaves had piled
like sad brown frogs.

Approximate Frog

Six in a jam jar.
Approximate frog swallows two,
becomes more of himself than he was;
munches one with three legs
and a web-footed stump.

Approximate frog looks around: We are
  three.
Not at all what we were,
but I'm me. Me. Me.

Approximate frog palps and mashes
available flesh.
Is a trio of meat,
grown green from the grass of his tribe.
Complete.

Horror

At the bottom of the cellar stairs
It was suddenly not all right.
Sent for Corona from the wooden crate
I stopped. Up in the shop my father served
Another customer and waited for the
  lemonade.

I saw the cheeses, huge and white as moons,
I saw the stacks of cans and barrelled lard,
The grating where the daylight leaked
  through ferns
And there they were. Two long pale frogs.
  Glistening.
Jewels on the dark stone flags. Tender,
  waxy,
Not emerald or malachite, but something
  sudden,
Clammy and alive with unexpected
  flutterings of skin.

And were there more of them? I felt the dread
Rise in me and was afraid to tread another step.
Underneath the darkness at my feet the stone
Could suddenly be soft as yoghurt.
I did not want to hurt them.
In my heart I saw them dead.
Heard the sickly split of seaweed bladders bursting in my head.

'They won't hurt you. See?' My mother stroked
Their backs to make them hop, but I was frozen.
Their slithery spring, their shocking length of legs
Appalled me. Their rawness terrified me, I feared
The crunch of shell-like bone, the awful stickiness of eggs.

Meltis

Outside the sweetshop he blinked.
  Swallowed.
The butterscotch in gold paper winked
Remarkably like the eyes of an Antean frog.
The whole place was eyes
In jars,
Small creatures in bottles,
And liquorice like the stringy gills
Of his sister species on Centauri.
Oh, the fizz of sherbet
Fuzzed as the stinging mist of mating airflies
The cherry lips, the satin cushions
Spoke to him of other skins.
He wished for home.

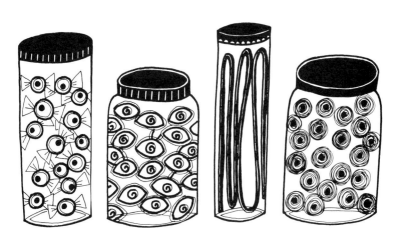

Against the odds he took a box of
　Meltis Fruits
And watched them sugar sparkle
In the nest he made for them.
Thought of their liquid centres
Wet as eggs.
Blinked. Swallowed.
Turned on the bulb that hung above them.
Dreamed of their improbable
Desirable
Sweet
Sweet
Hatching.

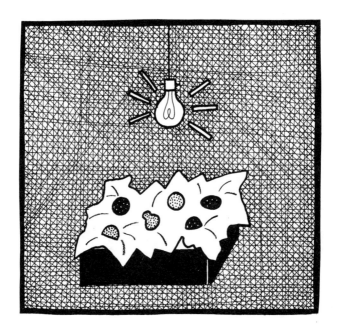

Big Fish

Here comes Bubblemouth with his one wide
   eye.
Shark black and sleeky skinned,
Tank-backed and feet finned.
Here comes Bubblemouth – poke, poke, pry.

Rubbery ribbony, lazy leathery,
Watching, waiting – I.

Here comes Bubblemouth with his peeping
   tom arm.
Rooting and fingering.
Lifting rocks, lingering.
Watch out Bubblemouth, I mean you harm.

I'm a tunnel with teeth in it,
Want your flesh – the beef in it.

So sidle slidle this way,
Choose this cave crack. Swim-sway.
Easy does it, child's play.
I watch, flat-eyed, grim grey.

This is my world. You trespass
Sucking bottles of sky gas.

Sea tolerates you where you think that you conquer,
Think you have mastery, believe you're the stronger.
But inside this rock I am lither and longer.
Mile of muscle. Hunger. Conger.

Ho ho, Bubblemouth, gently float
Then feel my teeth meet in your throat.

Windows

I looked through windows made of ice
And saw the swarms of silver fish
Flutter and flick away. Zig, zig
Through water white as albumen,
Water green as frozen spears.

I looked through windows made of leaves
Where paintbox parrots scream and flap
Where emerald snakes seem limbs of vines
Siss, wind and slide in strangling creepers.
Where bees and dragons burn and sting
While blood red flowers eat the steaming air.

I looked through windows made of bread
And saw the yellow eyes of men
Saw too many yellow bones
The yellow hunger of their skin.
They stood in long slow lines and starved
I saw them there, but didn't let them in.

Elephant

The hunters came and took you
From your mother in the dark
Her ribcage hooped and bloody
Like a meaty Noah's Ark
The termites eating what they could
The fireflies' bitter spark danced on your
   dead mother
In the jungle of her heart.

Oh, elephant. Ah, elephant,
Placid on your pad of stone.
Tusked and steaming in the hot night
Penned up here where you have grown.
Oh, elephant. Ah, elephant,
Through the trapdoor of the dark
Dream your way to Africa from the
   nightmare of the park.

Tramp

He'd a wrinkly face and shaky hands
And his shoulders hunched up high.
His wispy hair was a haze of grey,
The cold wind watered his eyes.
We watched him hobble
And we called him names, then dodged his stick –
Played spin-dizzy games . . .

He was old and weird and he made us wild.
His hop-dip step called the wicked child
That each of us keeps locked inside.
He wasn't like adults were supposed to be –
If he broke the rules, then so could we.

And he died in the park by the witch's hat.
On his own. I keep remembering that.

Fat Ladies in the Cinema

They always find me, fat ladies in the cinema,
Who lose umbrellas and then root,
Flipping up each smelly seat in turn –
Red plush that whing-thump-ticks in sequence.
Scratchy dominoes.
We clutch our coats and handbags, hats to laps,
'Excuse me, dear', and 'sorry', down the line.
The squash of fleshy hips and stomach
Making for the aisle.

After ice-cream, umbrella still adrift
She comments on the film:
'It's ketchup that. Oo, what's he doing now?
He's going in the back room, going down the stairs,
D.Y.N.A.M.I. – Ooo! Well fancy!
Wasn't he that doctor on the telly? And him so nice,
Who'd have thought he'd turn a murderer?'
Then missing bits, not understanding twists:
'But I thought he was with the other one . . .
Do have a nut, no do. I've plenty left.'
The wrapping crackles through the lovers' final kiss.
The row in front, incensed at last,
Turns round and blames *me* with a long held hiss.

Aunt Ellen's Bed

Aunty Ellen had a Yorkshire pudding bed.
A feather mattress that she sank into,
That rose around her like white leavened dough
Swelling in soft hills: she snuggled
Like a sausage toad.
And once or twice I slept there too,
Shared the fluffed pillows that wrapped my head;
Muffled all the noises of the house
And muted the twang of bedsprings, coiled as swarf,
Mysterious ringlets underneath that deep and downy bed.

Waiting For

This is the year of the money box
When Mrs Da Sylva will play
At holidays and new expensive frocks.
This is the year of the money box.
The unlocking year. The year of Paris
And Los Angeles and rubies big as rocks.
Oh, Mrs Da Sylva, cunning as the fox
And thrifty; careful of the last sweet scrape
   of jam,
Careful as the clever darning of worn socks,
Is taking a hammer to her money box.
Sick of saving, sick of prudent locks,
Dreaming of cruise ships waiting in the
   docks.
Mrs Da Sylva's time has come at last:
Box smithereened. Box withereened.
No more bacon boiled and butterbeaned.
For this is the year
       this is the year
       this is the year
              of the money box.

Edward

Edward, sixty, lived in the house he built
  himself –
Screened and wound about by woods,
The footpaths muffled by the strangling
  undergrowth.
He had no visitors.
No signposts, so he had to burn the rubbish
And collect the mail.
So when he upped and went to South
  America
There was no one to notice.
Till, on his return,
He started coming down the hill –
Drank shorts, then, careful for his liver,
Pints of lime juice.
On bonfire night he asked us back
For fireworks better than the town display.

There was a wall of deathmasks,
Taboo faces from Peru,
And guns.
We ate his pizzas, drank the punch
Chewed nervously on little coffins made of marzipan
And then saw pickled snakes, dried spiders
As we searched for the loo.
'Every window's armour-plated glass,' he said
And passed the salad.
This information changed our calculations
As we fought through brambles
On our way back to the road.

The Unlucky Baker

I bake the bread for harvest –
White flour laced with arsenic
So nibbling mice that fringe
The surplices and cassocks die
And dessicate beside the heating ducts.
A neat trick taught me by a priest
Who hated cats.
He it was who gave the tainted rice
To shower about the shining brides.
Churchyard pigeons streak the headstones.
   Make mess.
And is not old confetti ugly after rain?
He had me plug the air gaps in the organ loft
Then when our faulty gas pipes leaked
Bade me sweep the dead bats rustling in a
   heap.
I remember their soft fur, the rough hessian
   of the sack.
He didn't die of injuries sustained
When falling from a pulpit crumbling
With deathwatch beetle.

But he should have done.

Roy's Dance

As it used to be. In white.
A jacket and long apron tied about his waist.
He'd dip the fish in batter
Slip it to the fat, the vat of hot oil,
Then shiver all the chips free of their
　bubbling.
Never still.
All dip and step and shake the drips,
Beaded and afloat between the crisping
　fillets.
Never still.
The queue moved as Roy presided at the
　range.
He'd take a cloth and wipe a spot – invisible –
Invisibly away. He didn't turn, return
The greetings of the few who knew him well
　enough to say,
But nodded in the mirror, an 'evening'.
Dip, side-step, sidle of the hips;
Roy's dance.

And the old girls now
Who stop to chat with mothers
Watching children ride their bikes,
Remember how it was before he sold the shop.
Before they modernized.
It's smarter now. And dearer –
The stainless isn't loved. How could it be?
They're only boys . . .
It's clean, but where's the *gleam*?
And Roy's stroke has changed his step.
The dance is not the same.

Ghosts in Our Suburban Homes

The creaking of a wicker chair
When something unseen settles there.
It's ghosts, ss, ss, ss,
It's ghosts.
Mad wardrobes swinging in the night,
A flicker at the edge of sight,
It's ghosts, ss, ss, ss,
It's ghosts.
The rocker rocks. The curtains sigh.
Out of the corner of your eye
The solid darkness passes by,
It's ghosts!

They spread themselves along the wall,
Shadows with shadows haunt the hall,
A great grey silent waterfall
Of ghosts!

Come midnight, watch the stair-
Tread sink with no foot there.
It's ghosts, ss, ss, ss,
It's ghosts.
A thousand thousand whispering souls
Mass quietly behind small holes.
A million slither through the cracks
Behind the door, behind our backs,
Insinuating white as wax
Are ghosts!

And in the silence of the moon,
The silver silence of the moon,
The ghosts release a silent tune
To rise like steam from some sad tomb.
The soundless song of frozen skies,
The ice of unsung lullabies,
Wordless as the frosted eyes
Of ghosts.

Ghosts in our suburban homes.
Ghosts in our suburban homes.
Ghosts, ss, ss, ss,
Ghosts.

No More Socks

No More Socks:
I'm sick of them. Give me an earthquake
Wrapped in lava glittery as foil and bright as marmalade.

                      Give me cataclysms
Wrapped in the sound of a thousand cymbals rolling
Down a mountainside, ribboned with lightning
And the plasma of exploding stars.

                    Give me cataracts, torrents,
Raging water, white as blizzards tied up with jungles
Parcelled with the emerald arms of glamorous vines.

Not socks, not teatowels: thunder, peacocks, diamonds,
The breathing ocean, constellations. Trees
Pouring green and dizzy from the middle of the spinning earth.

Advice to the Horticulturalist

Sing into the trumpet of the amaryllis,
Read lists of numbers to the clematis,
Recite long poems to the patient cactus,
But whisper, whisper to the hyacinth.

Science fiction for the spider plant,
Victorian sermons for the pyracanth.
A hellebore will relish murder
Mock orange has a taste for Thurber.
Avoid polemic near delphiniums –
They get the blight from fixed opinions.
Invective will not put things right
If weeds are rioting.
Nor will abuse be any use –
They like the frisson, flourish on the spite.

A weeping willow fed on secrets
Grows and grows and grows.
While golden rod and Russian vine
Enjoy experimental prose.
Forget-me-nots spread fast as gossip,
Don't tell a lily lies,
You can be risqué with a tulip,
A rose will thrive on sighs.

So sing into the trumpet of the amaryllis,
Spout logarithms to the clematis,
Recite your epic to the patient cactus,
But whisper, whisper to the hyacinth.

The Seven Brains of the Caterpillar

My first brain thinks the colour of my skin.
Dresses me as green as lettuce.
My second brain arranges crawling.
One slow sucker foot. Hump and wriggle.
Brain three says eat.
Four lullabies me.
Five dreams my breathing,
Lets the wet air suck sweetly in and out.
Six senses danger,
Rolls me up bud-tight at a touch
But seven lies still. Does nothing. Bides.
It will spin me my shroud, set me my coffin.
Pupa. Pupa. Sound it like a pulse.
From this dead shell I will be born again
A butterfly. An angel.

Marcello Malpighi's Theory

In every egg another tiny human
Male or female, according to the plan.
In every girl another preformed person
Each a furled woman or a fist-tight man.
The dead and gone, the unborn still to come
Slept in Mother Eve's egg, every one.

This Russian-doll design means that 'forever'
Is not what is intended for our race.
We calculate the limits of creation
By numbering the lives packed in that space.
So live life slowly.
Slowly, let the generations pass.
What will they not dare, not do, those final
 children,
Knowing themselves empty and the last?

Note: Marcello Malpighi (1628–94) was an Italian anatomist.

The Barber-Surgeon at Avebury

I am here
in the third blade of grass from the left,
and here in the trip-you-up tree root.
Some of me
lurks in yellow lichen.

It isn't what I meant.
I meant to die
insignificant
in my own bed,
in my own house,
> – the kitchen smelling
> of iron pans and mackerel
> the bedroom of elderflowers –

but everyone knew
the stones
were the work of the devil.
It was duty, you see,
dragged me into this.

> We went out righteous;
> spades and psalms
> would do it.

Each of us took turns
to dig the pit.
I blistered – more used to scissors
than a spade.
'Look,' I said
and spread my hand into the sun
that warmed the ready grave.
The women laughed,
said I was soft as leeches,
that hard work never hurt a man.

The blacksmith lifted Catherine with one hand.

In the middle of the jokes
the sarsen fell

> – green sky
> green earth
> green stone
> the sapling by the ditch
> fat Catherine's laugh
> the crumbs of soil
> roll, rolling down
> the damp smell
> and the feel of dirt –

The boasting muscles froze.

The stone was heavy
Nothing for it but to leave me
buried with the pagan.

In my own home,
in my own bed,
no one would have wondered.

I meant to die
    quietly, without fuss,
    to hear the click of beads
and be forgotten.

But I am here.
Pinned by the stone,
held in the grass.

Fast in memory
alive in eyes
that watch the lichen
on the yellow stone.

Note: In medieval times, and earlier, people tried to destroy or bury the stones of Avebury Ring, a stone circle much bigger and older than Stonehenge, because they believed them to be evil. During excavations in 1938 archaeologists found the skeleton of a man who had been accidentally killed during the 'burial' of a stone in the fourteenth century. A leather pouch and its contents indicate that he was a barber-surgeon.

Holme Fen

In 1848 they pushed a pillar in the fen.
Stuck it like a giant pin down fifteen feet
Into the buttery clay. The head sat flush in
 fenland peat.

Today the post and pillar stand
In full view. Even the concrete plinth
Is proud above the land. Holme Fen is
 withering.
The peat is drying like a browning raisin.

It is a quiet place.
Here where the earth has shrunk,
The feet that stood beside the mere in '48
 dance silently
Amongst the leaves. Memories do not touch
 us
They are in the hands of topmost twigs
That scratch the wide East Anglian sky.

The past once happened high above our
   heads.
And long before they sucked the sea away
This land was something else again.
The wind that stirs the bracken and the reeds
Is grey and moist as souls of fenland eels.
The silver air moves past us
Like the ghosts of cold-flanked fish.

Choosing

'He's nice. Oh, look at him!' – My mother's
   voice
About the baby boy whose red hair marked
   him out
From all the others in the line of cots.
The first part of my special story,
Told before I knew what words were.
Heard well. And over, over once again,
Whenever spots or fever tangled sleep
She'd tell about that boy who'd tempted her,
That red-haired boy, the one they almost had
Before they found the small fat baby,
   sleeping.
– Ah, and then she opened those big eyes,
Big blue eyes just like dad's, and laughed.
And 'That's the one,' he said. –
My story goes like that. They picked me,
Not that golden baby with the shining hair.
I know I'm loved.
Why is it then I buy, quite regularly,
Tubes of 'Chestnut Glow' or henna from the
   chemist's shop?

Sunday School Sports

Soon. Soon.
Any minute now it'll be the egg and spoon.
Run. Run.
It doesn't matter if you lose – it's only done for fun.
Lies. Lies.
The winner is the one who gets the prize,
The loser gets a slow-hand clap and then sits down and cries.
Cheat. Cheat.
I hear the awful chanting and I trip on my own feet.

Dumb. Dumb.
I really didn't know you couldn't grip it with your thumb . . .

Olympic Diver

After the long straight climb I walk the
 plank.
It should sing – taut and tender as the
 wounded string
Of a violin. Still and high. I stand.
Breathe.
It is time for transformation.
I gather myself – feet curl to talons,
Calves, thighs muscled like a bird's to the
 spring,
I fly. Up and out into the above.
Shift into a coil. Spin, straighten, fold and
 open,
Serpent to arrow entering the plummet.
I am molten, a tear of dropping lead.
I fall and water opens for me. No splash.
We are the same – water to water.
I eel in a line of silver. Broken bubbles
Scatter, run with me.
And then the gathering again.
Flick.
I am in air. Still
Beside the still green square. Listen.
In the silence is triumph.
The gentle ebb is proof of magic.
All is as it was.

Uniform

'You'll grow,' she said and that was that. No use
To argue and to sulk invited slaps.
The empty shoulders drooped, the sleeves hung loose –
No use – she nods and the assistant wraps.

New blazer, new school socks and all between
Designed for pea pod anonymity.
All underwear the regulation green;
Alike there's none to envy, none to pity.

At home she feasts on pins. She tacks and tucks
Takes in the generous seams and smiles at thrift.
I fidget as she fits. She tuts and clucks.
With each neat stitch she digs a deeper rift.

They'll mock me with her turnings and her hem
And laugh and know that I'm not one of them.

Nearly Thirteen

I'm nearly thirteen and my name isn't Mary,
It's Lola. I'm wild and exotic and mean.
My mum's not my real mum. My mother's a gypsy
And one day she'll claim me and I'll be their queen.

The people I live with don't understand me.
They don't seem to realize I am unique.
I'm going to be famous and sinful and blasé,
As soon as they let me out nights in the week.

I want to wear satin and black fishnet stockings.
I want feather boas and glittering rings.
One eye on the mirror, I practise seductions,
And plan the sensation peroxide will bring.

I want it all now. I want it to happen.
I am Mata Hari and Brigitte Bardot.
All they can think of is cabbage and homework,
When I want a party they always say no.

They think I'm a kid. I fight them. I lose.
God, I wish I had breasts and could wear high-heel shoes.

The Jam and Bread Test

In our house we'd the jam and bread test.
'I'm hungry,' wouldn't do, not by itself.
You had to be plain hungry,
Not hungry for a peach, a plum;
Your hunger had to be a hole in you
A great wide gap to stuff with wodges of white bread.
There was no room for fancy. We were *sensible*.
If tea was stew, but you were pudding hungry,
You'd no chance. Not stew? She'd look at you
– A glance that lances like a laser beam –
'Right, jam and bread then.' That was it.
You couldn't shift and shuffle sausages around
And hope for jelly with an uncleaned plate.
You couldn't be too tired for washing up
But wide awake enough for telly.
Time enough to play a game was time enough
To finish homework, tidy up, clean shoes.
You could get nothing past my lovely, stern and cuddly mum.
I always failed the jam and bread test.

Barbara in the Shed

That wasn't how it happened.
We told them we hadn't meant to do it.
I'm good at lies. I know to mix them in with truth.
My dad's a brickie and I understand cement.
We never meant to lock her in.
The door stuck. I was playing with the bolt,
It cut my finger, look. I lead them off the scent
With blood and rust, a feathered flap of skin.
Busy them with Savlon and Elastoplast.
'I'm sorry if we made her cry.' Another lie,
But sugared – her tears swamped by mine.
We'd loved it. Poking and stretching our faces into fangs.
And when we pushed her in the shed we danced
And hammered triumph on the walls.
That's the way it was.

In the Meantime

When my best friend moved back to town
I visited. They had a bigger house now,
In a smarter part. Her dad was more important
Than before. He had his picture in the paper.

I wanted . . . something. I wasn't really sure,
I only knew I needed . . . something.
It was a shock to see her. She was tall and thin
Long-haired, dark-eyed and glamorous.

I took a present for her little sister,
A doll I'd kept and cosied in a drawer
Her hair still pretty and the dresses
Neat and proper. Clean as new.

My best friend was a stranger.
Her sister drew in biro on the doll.
And everything was wasted.
When I went home, my mum was cross.

A Serious Talk

My father stops my teasing with a look.
I've run that way before, but not this time.
He stands his ground determined, I consent.
He holds the box I've known for all my life
– the secrets box kept hidden in the loft –
Shows me the key, kept in another place,
And then the envelope with deeds and wills.
'Solicitors are best. They'll sort it out.
You need do nothing, only give them this.'
I nod, the safest answer I can give,
Shore up the surge of words, hold back the slide.
How businesslike he seems, prepared and calm,
Explaining, underlining, making clear.
The loose ends of his life combed flat, laid out
Put tidy in manila and mahogany.
'We'll not be buried, burning's best.' He says,
'We'll be cremated, both of us.'
Oh years ago we used to scrub the graves
Of aunts and grandmas, sweep and scour the stones,

Rake straight the chippings, weed the narrow paths,
Throw out the stagnant water and old wreaths.
No one takes buckets to the churchyard now.
Their choice accuses me, says stark and plain
There's no use planning on a well-kept plot.
Be dust and done with rather than display
Neglect in death. Decay broadcasts decay.

They opt for ashes, shun a run-down grave.
I listen to it all. Say nothing still.
My mother rescues me with jokes, smiles, wry,
'Don't fancy worms. Don't fancy flames.' Decides,
'Don't think I'll bother dying after all!'
And then we laugh, my father too, but then
Forbids escape again: 'You'll not forget?
The box, the key –' 'The envelope,' I say.
And speech confirms me in my father's world.
Acknowledged, real for ever from these words.
No mocking now, no, nothing I can say
Will alter it, or make it go away.

Heart Stuff

Mums and dads they tell you all this stuff
And some of it's OK and some of it is guff.
There's the fairy who takes teeth – that's a story and a half
A sort of magic dentist; gives you cash for fangs – a laugh.
This Father Christmas thing – you know the score –
I've looked out for him, I've squinted out of duvets,
Pretended sleep, but kept watch on the door,
But still I've never seen him. Never will,
My mother says. This Christmas thing, this Jesus stuff
That's strange stuff. Big stuff. After all, a star . . .
. . . Not every baby gets a welcome from the sky.

It makes you wonder. Makes you cry
To think what happened then.
If you ask me, I'd say he had it rough.
If he was all that meek and mild, how come he was so tough?
Dads and mums they tell you stuff,
Some sticks and some goes in one ear, then out.
They go on, don't they? My mum can't half shout.
But some stuff's special, like this Christmas thing.
You hear it in your heart . . . sounds daft – it's not, you know:
I keep remembering a marvellous baby in the shining snow.

Angels

We are made from light.
Called into being we burn
brighter than the silver-white
Of hot magnesium.
More sudden than yellow phosphorus.
We are the fire of heaven;
Blue flames and golden ether.

We are from stars.
Spinning beyond the farthest galaxy
In an instant gathered to this point
We shine, speak our messages then go,
Back to the brilliance.
We are not separate, not individual,
We are what we are made of. Only
Shaped sometimes into tall-winged warriors,
Our faces solemn as swords,
Our voices joy.

The skies are cold;
Suns do not warm us;
Fire does not burn itself.
Only once we touched you
And felt a human heat.
Once, in the brightness of the frost.
Above the hills, in glittering starlight,
Once, we sang.